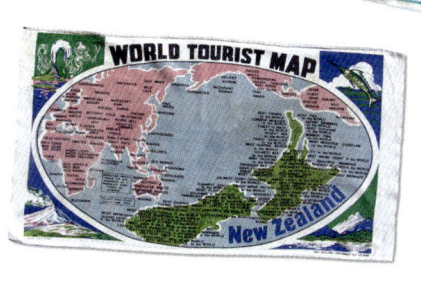

Every Tea Towel Tells a Story

Richard Till's Special Collection

Every Tea Towel Tells a Story

Richard Till's Special Collection

First published in 2010 by Renaissance Publishing, Auckland
PO Box 56 716, Dominion Road, Auckland 1446, New Zealand
rl@renaissancepublishing.co.nz

1 3 5 7 9 10 8 6 4 2

Copyright in text: © 2010 Richard Till
Copyright: © 2010 Renaissance Publishing

The right of Richard Till to be identified as the author of this work in terms of section 96 of the Copyright Act 1994 is hereby asserted.

ISBN: 978-0-9864521-0-9

A catalogue record for this book is available from the National Library of New Zealand

Photography and book design: Trevor Newman

This book is copyright. Except for the purpose of fair reviewing, no part of this publication may be reproduced, stored in a retrieval system, or transmitted in any form or by any means, electronic, mechanical, photocopying, recording or otherwise, without the prior permission of the publishers and copyright holders. Infringers of copyright render themselves liable to prosecution.

Printed in China through Bookbuilders

Introduction

I've always cooked with a tea towel over my shoulder. They are very handy to handle things hot from the oven, to clean the rims of plates before service and best of all they are plentiful and easily washed. When I came to make the television cooking series *Kiwi Kitchen* for TVOne, I threw one of the two old Kiwiana tea towels I owned at that time over my shoulder during the first couple of episodes. Suddenly it seemed like a good idea to have a different one each week, and to make a feature of it. The popular tea towel of the week segment was born and I began to collect what is now a ridiculously large number of them. It seems to me that of all the addictions I could have, this is probably one of the least harmful.

Richard Till

More Than Just a Map

A classic tea towel design with its map showing regional highlights featured as close as possible to where they might be found. This particular tea towel is my favourite rendition of the genre, not least because the map is so anatomically suggestive with its out-of-scale mountainous lumps in all the right places. But it's the coastline that I reckon is the real winner. The oceans lap against an even-sized embankment that runs around the whole coast, making the country seems satisfyingly anchored and solid. I'm proud to say I've stood in front of every scenic attraction highlighted, although my closest brush with the mountain in Taranaki was after its name change from Mt Egmont.

Hutton's: The No. 1 Choice

I remember when this Hutton's range appeared on supermarket shelves. I remember desperately, but ultimately hopelessly, wanting my mother to buy our sausages and saveloys this way, packaged and shrink-wrapped, rather than folded in brown paper and then packed within the big bundle of meat from the butcher, which usually had a little blood oozing out one corner and was tied up with string.

Packaged food looked far more exciting than the stuff that came from the family garden or in unmarked bags and wrappings. To me, as a child, packaged food seemed modern and exciting. I think the first packet food we ate was rice risotto. I remember watching in wonder as my mother tipped in the mysterious flavouring powder. It was a Sunday night and we were listening to the story playing on National Radio, which was *The Hound of the Baskervilles*. To this day, whenever I eat packet rice risotto, I can hear that hound howling.

Nowadays everything's turned on its head and there's nothing nicer than a string of sausages in brown paper.

FOOD,
GLORIOUS
FOOD...
Hutton's
SWAN
PORK SAUSAGES
Hutton's
HAM & EGG
Hutton's
BEEF SAUSAGES
Hutton's
HAM & CHICKEN
FLAVOUR
demand
(and see that you get)
Hutton's
SAVELOYS
Hutton's
GARLIC
Hutton's
BLACK PUDDING
Hutton's
FRANKFURTS
Hutton's
PORK BRAWN
Hutton's
PORK
CHIPOLATAS
Hutton's
SAVOURY
LUNCH
NO.1 CHOICE EVERYWHERE!

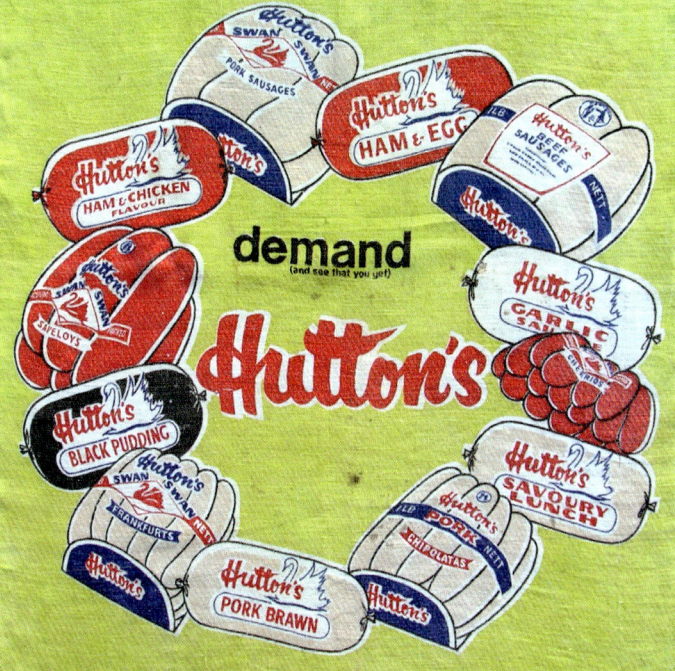

Auckland Harbour Bridge

In days gone by anything new, exciting or even deemed worthy enough was honoured by having a tea towel made to celebrate its arrival or, in the case of the Auckland Harbour Bridge, its construction. On this particular subject it seems that the commemorative tea towel was a highly competitive market because I know of at least two other tea towels made to mark the grand new harbour crossing.

   I'm especially fond of this one because it paints a strangely bucolic picture of Auckland, all rolling green hills with barely a building in sight. I assume that's because hills without buildings were easier to paint and print. It's also a favourite because of the peculiar perspective of the bridge and the ship passing near it, but most of all for the wonderful rendering of the clouds.

   Over recent years I've had the honour of having my likeness replicated on more than one fund-raising tea towel created by a particular community group for which I've done a show. All I'll say is that this rendition of the Auckland Harbour Bridge is more flattering than any of the pictures of me.

Hawke's Bay Hot Spots

Although I've been to Hawke's Bay many times I have yet to tangle with any of the dizzy array of hot spots featured here. Any tea towel that featured the memorable highlights of my Hawke's Bay experiences would look very different – there'd be a beautifully constructed bacon and egg pie available from the bowls club, a brass band marching competition, a waterfront motel room with a gigantic spa pool just inches away from the bed, a meal at a Thai restaurant with a bishop and – from long, long ago – the poor mistreated dolphins at Marineland. All very colourful, just like this one. But because of the printing costs it's unlikely anyone would make my Hawke's Bay tea towel. Most modern ones are printed in only one or two colours.

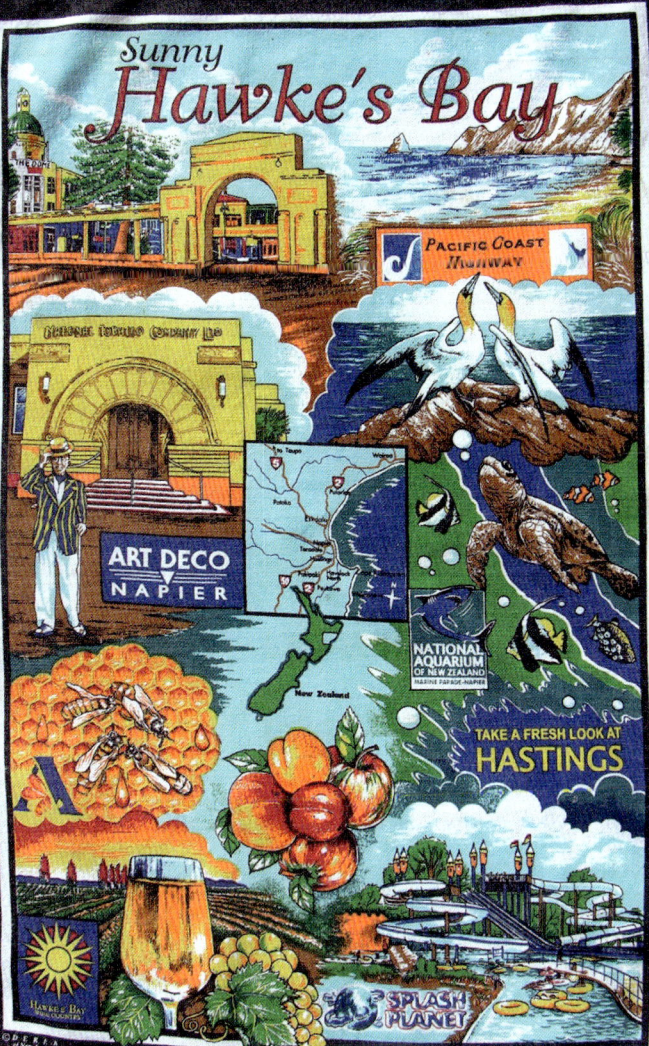

Cup of Tea, Anyone?

It's New Zealand's first time at the World Cup Finals so, OK, let's design a tea towel! It was made by arrangement with the NZFA World Cup Committee so there's probably a 'clean stadiums' joke in there somewhere, but I can't find it. I'm sure no tea towel was produced for the 2010 cup finals though, thus denying New Zealanders the chance to express their surges of football patriotism while drying the teacups (assuming anyone dries teacups anymore…). I actually got this tea towel from Perth.

Capital Spot

I have a great fondness for Wellington. Owned my first house there, our daughter was born there and I stumbled into professional cookery there. I'm not entirely sure how old this tea towel is, but it's clear there's no Te Papa, so by that – and other absences from the skyline – my guess is that it dates back to the mid 1970s. The artist has chosen to represent the city on a summer afternoon, with dry patches of grass on the playing fields by the University and the lowering sun falling on the distant Rimutakas. By adding the scuds of northerly cloud an effort's been made to keep it climatologically realistic, but I think the mental picture of the city in the imagination of anyone who loves Wellington is of those few still, cloudless days that show the city at its beautiful best.

Decorative Yet Practical

The summers of my childhood had a soundtrack of radio commentary of Plunket Shield Cricket matches. Back then Central and Northern Districts were much harder teams for me to imagine than Canterbury, Otago, Auckland and Wellington – and because of that it just seemed wrong on the occasions that Canterbury was beaten by one of those geographically vague teams. I've no idea when the cricket associations started adding animals and wizards to their sense of identity, but it's clear that this tea towel comes from the early days of Central District's association with the stag. It's nice use of two colour printing and would have looked spanking in the bar of many a cricket club throughout the centre of the North Island and a good number of them must have wiped the inside of many a jug and pint glass.

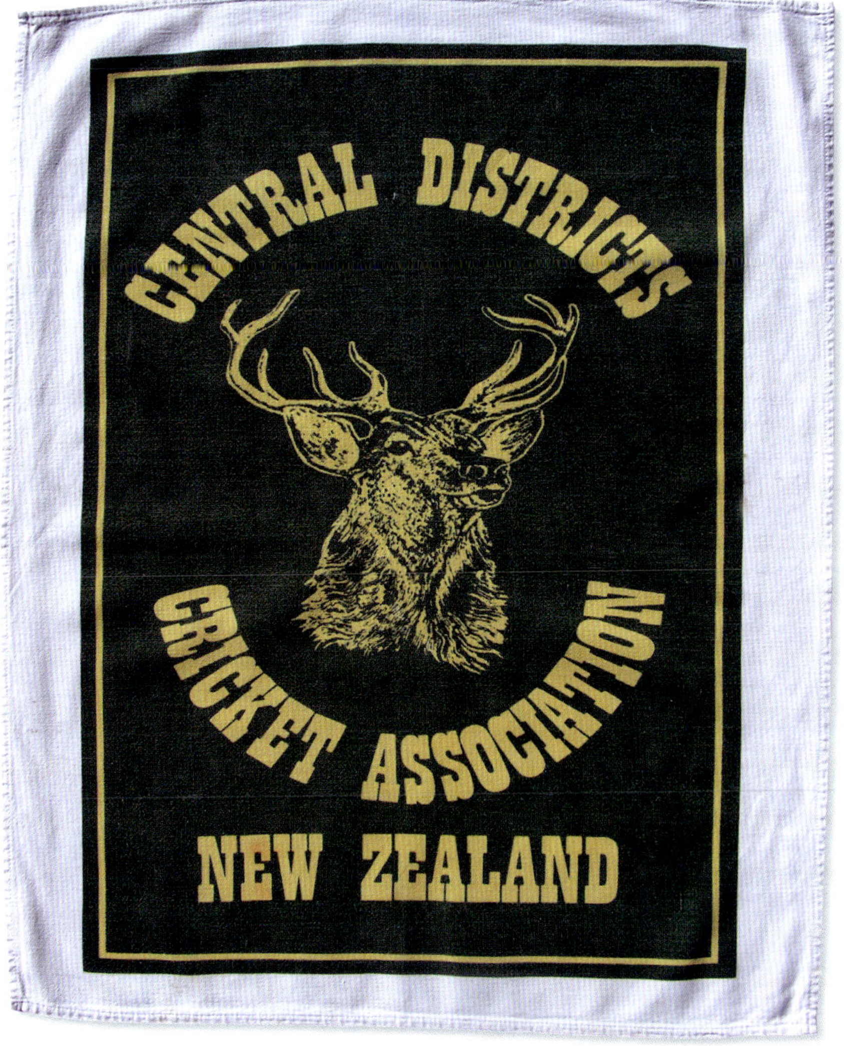
CENTRAL DISTRICTS
CRICKET ASSOCIATION
NEW ZEALAND

All That Glitters …

Although I recall that in July 1981 I was working at the Court Theatre in Christchurch, my only memories of this famous wedding relate to the closure of the theatre for the occasion because the television broadcast kept every possible theatre-goer at home glued to the screen. Another memory is of a bunch of us getting drunk at a local 'wedding party' hosted by one of the Court actors. He was a very camp gentleman and I recall him wearing a bridal veil and crying profusely during the vows, then predicting that it would all end badly. It's a pretty spectacular tea towel and the only one I own that features sparkling gold ink. A gilded tea towel indeed.

Graphic Wonderland

It might seem too far-fetched for people with any idea about the comparison I'm about to make, but this tea towel reminds me of some etchings from the *Book of Job* by William Blake (published in 1826). The similarity is that the images appear within the mouth of the surrounding image that is itself rendered by scale into being a patterned border. The hand-drawn type utilised to create the words 'Wonderland of New Zealand Rotorua' (most particularly the 'W') gives it a style all of its own as well as a sort of enthusiastic, clumsy energy. It's my absolute favourite single colour tea towel.

Boyhood Memories

When I was eight I accompanied my father on a tour around the North Island. In Rotorua we visited the geysers, were mesmerised by boiling mud, saw Maori boys diving off a bridge to retrieve coins thrown into the water by tourists and marvelled at the huge rainbow trout that we fed with some pellets bought in a little white paper bag exactly the same as a 10c mixture would have come in. I came home with a little Maori carving that is still lurking in the back of one of the drawers in my desk. It was my first exposure to tourist activity and, coming from a pakeha private school background, my first exposure to anything Maori. For me this tea towel sums up those memories (plus a gondola), nicely rendered in a very simple block colour style.

ROTORUA
GONDOLA AND
LAKE ROTORUA
RAINBOW AND
BROWN TROUT
HAERE MAI
GOVERNMENT GARDENS
POHUTU GEYSER
WHAKAREWAREWA
MAORI CARVING
ST. FAITHS CHURCH
OHINEMUTU
NEW ZEALAND

So Much More than Beautiful

Feilding is the epicentre of my exposure to the Keep New Zealand Beautiful campaign. I visited Feilding to perform in a food and wine festival and met local powerhouse Del Gibb, a major player in the Keep New Zealand Beautiful Campaign.

When the campaign began in 1979 with the New Zealand Litter Act, Del attended a meeting as a representative of the Girl Guides and was elected as chair of the Feilding Committee. Under her guidance Feilding has been voted New Zealand's most beautiful town 14 times. I've since worn my Keep Feilding Beautiful apron with great pride. As you can see here the town is much more than beautiful anyway; there's also motor racing at Manfield, a clock tower, a steam railway society, Kowhai Park and a bronze sculpture of a farmer and his dog. And as it says, it's friendly.

A Bargain at the Price

This tea towel claims that Pakatoa Island used to be the holiday hub of the Hauraki Gulf. There was a friendly fraternity, a heated swimming pool, chalets for family comfort and, of course, golden beaches. At the time of writing Pakatoa Island is also for sale. It's the largest privately owned island in the gulf and for $40 million this island (with 62 bedrooms and 62 bathrooms) could be yours. Maybe this congruence of events suggests there's a future for tea towels in real estate marketing.

A Stylish Effort

While this rather beautiful tea towel was designed to be a fundraiser for sure, its paper doll graphic artfully displays the bond linking rural women around the entire country with real style and meaning to boot. The succinct contact details for the national office, support activities of the organisation and resources for members also gives it some functional message, but for me it's really just a beautiful design in beautiful colours.

Halcyon Days

I've always loved illustrated nature guides, be they relating to fishes, trees or birds of New Zealand, but in my youth I would have had no time whatsoever for a tea towel version. But what a brilliant idea for the holiday home, bach or crib. Hang it over the kitchen towel rail and you're not only ready to do the dishes but also to identify the local fauna. This one, part of a fundraising series for Save the Children, prompts my favourite fun fact about the kingfisher, a bird I've only ever seen at too great a distance to fully admire its shimmering blue plumage. Apparently the expression 'halcyon days' refers to a bird in Greek mythology, now considered to be the kingfisher, which was capable of calming the seas for a short period in the depth of winter in order to lay her eggs.

Going, Going, Gone

There is very little that can be said about this. It represents a view of an archetypal New Zealand Man who's disappearing fast – I'll not offer an opinion about whether that's a good or a bad thing. Although he is the cornerstone of New Zealand folklore, you'll not find many young New Zealand men aspiring to be him.

In any event, this tea towel is relatively rare given it's an unusually squared rectangle shape, has a pronounced waffle texture in the fabric and is rather stylishly drawn.

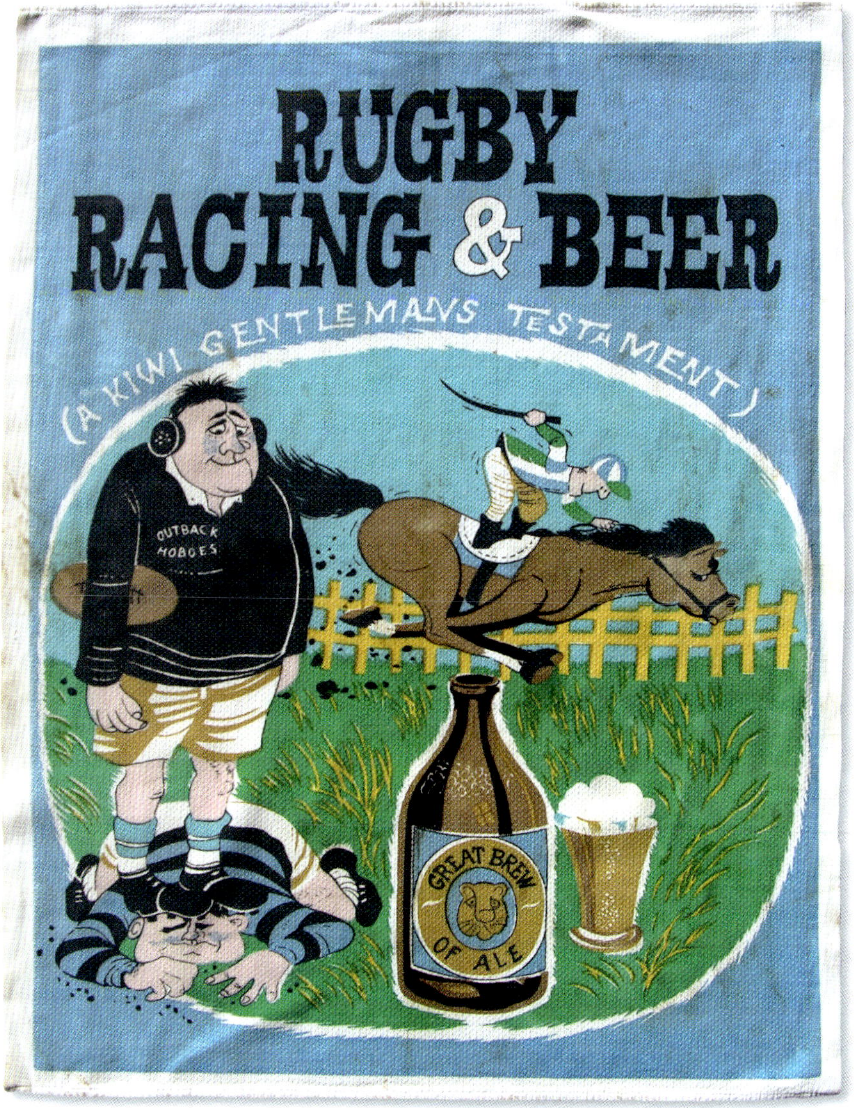
RUGBY
RACING & BEER
(A KIWI GENTLEMANS TESTAMENT)
OUTBACK HOBOES
GREAT BREW
OF ALE

Dollars and Cents

There were a goodly number of tea towels produced to educate the dish-drying public about the decimalisation of our currency on 10 July, 1967; this one is focused on the coins themselves. I remember the day being something of a headache for my mother. For me, it made no difference. I had no money to spend on the 9th and still none on the 10th, so the format of currency mattered little. Now that we've moved on from these coins this tea towel is somewhat nostalgic as well as attractive – even though the Queen looks particularly grim in the image on the reverse of those coins. Note the scholarly dollar in the bottom right.

NEW ZEALAND DECIMAL CURRENCY COINS

THE OBVERSE SIDE OF ALL COINS

50 CENTS

10 CENTS

2 CENTS

5 CENTS

1 CENT

20 CENTS

DECIMAL CONVERSION TABLE

Shillings & Pence	20/-	10/-	9/-	8/-	7/-	6/-
Dollars & Cents	2 Dollars	1 Dollar	90c	80c	70c	60c
5/-	4/-	3/-	2/-	1/-	11d	10d	9d
50c	40c	30c	20c	10c	9c	8c	8c
8d	7d	6d	5d	4d	3d	2d	1d
7c	6c	5c	4c	3c	2c	2c	1c

DECIMAL CURRENCY DAY MONDAY JULY 10th 1967

Made in Ireland　　Fast Colours　　All Pure Linen

Community Rules

The Country Women's Institute (now Women's Institute) movement began in Canada in 1897. And I can tell you that New Zealand has about 8000 members in 445 institutes within 50 federations.

The aims of the movement are:
- To unite the women of an area into a group with such a strong community spirit that, through their mutual interests, they will so broaden their horizons as Homemakers that the Institute motto 'For Home and Country' becomes a reality, both in the home and in the community.
- To foster handcrafts, choral, drama and other cultural activities.
- To encourage participation in community affairs and a concerned interest in all aspects of national life.

And, of course, to sell tea towels to help all this happen.

NEW ZEALAND
FOR HOME
CWI
TUI
WOOD PIGEON
KOWHAI
FLAX LILY
AUCKLAND
TUA-TARA
KEA
DUNEDIN
MITRE PEAK

Kiwis on the Land

Just in case you can't work out what this tea towel is trying to tell us it's labelled 'Rural New Zealand'. And the small type on the bottom right tells us it's number 2 in a series (I wish I had them all!) The grain harvest image indicates the likely age of the tea towel, and I'm not too sure the apple pickers of today are as cheerful or even of European descent, but there you have it. The two different greens in the colour scheme were a bold choice for the time as some probably argued that they didn't go together. Nevertheless, it's a very nice collection of what our imagined countryside might look like.

RURAL NEW ZEALAND

A Mountain By Any Other Name

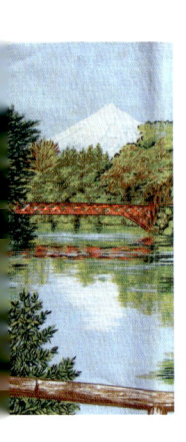

A magnificent clear day in the 'Naki. Personally, I've never experienced one, but it must happen every so often. This tea towel, old enough for the mountain to still be known as Mt Egmont, shows a beautiful vista across the water in New Plymouth's Pukekura Park, the home of the famous Brooklands Bowl where once, many years ago, a violinist in the orchestra which was accompanying my father in a concerto performance at the Bowl placed the leg of her chair too close to the edge of the stage and fell, mid concert, into the pond in front of the stage. I've always had a nice time in New Plymouth and I take every opportunity to visit. I'm sure if I go often enough, eventually I'll get to see the mountain clearly.

MT. EGMONT FROM PUKEKURA PARK, NEW PLYMOUTH, NEW ZEALAND.

A Bit of a Laugh

This tea towel is an elegant illustration of the confusion that exists in some people's mind between raunch culture and ranch culture. Or more particularly it represents the point where the two meet, with hilarious results. Well, either hilarious or sad or a poignant combination of the two. It's a bit of a tourist classic and provides Australians with plenty of ammunition for jokes from here until the end of time.

46   *Every Tea Towel Tells a Story*

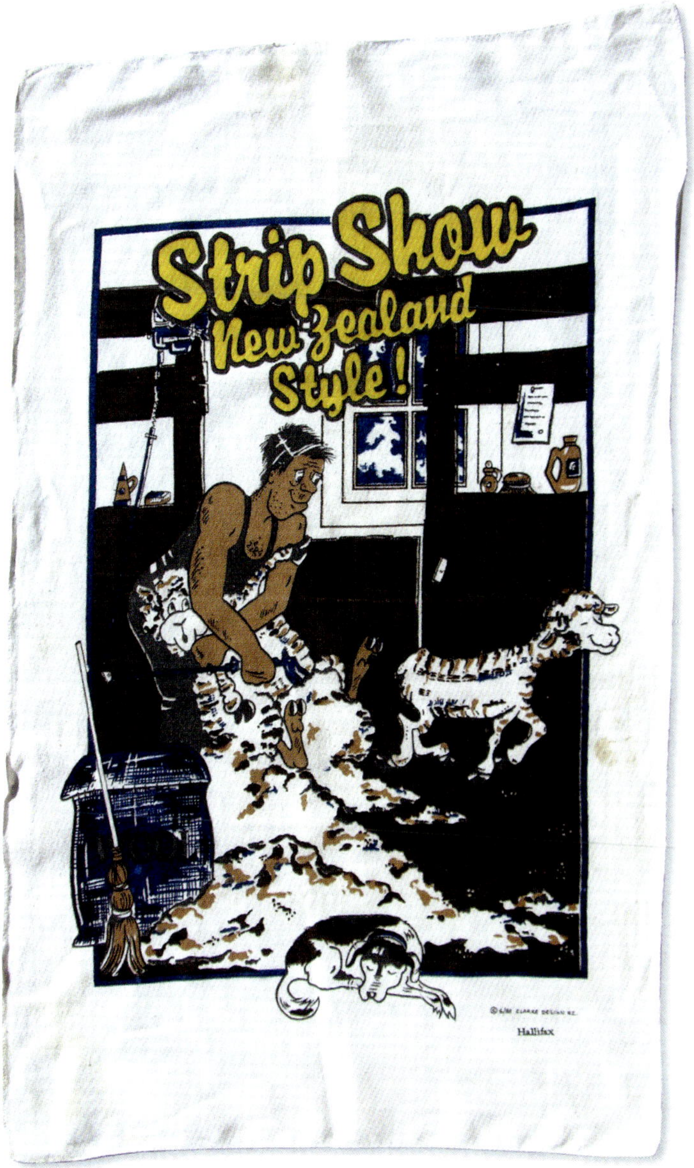
Strip Show
New Zealand
Style!
Hallifax

Keeping the Faith

As a child I just couldn't fathom the enthusiasm that everyone had for stamp collecting – all those stamp 'hinges', tweezers and album pages with bossy grid marking. Well, I get it now, and here are all the stamps that everyone wanted back then all on one (slightly faded) tea towel. To get this tea towel, I had to bid hard against a woman whom, I later discovered by way of a mutual friend, was trying to buy it so she could cut it up in order to sew stamps onto her young daughter's dress. This knowledge has made me double my efforts to buy all the good old tea towels I can find – to save them from the modern woman and her damn 'shabby chic' handcraft projects.

NEW ZEALAND
WHANGAREI
AUCKLAND
HAMILTON
TAURANGA
ROTORUA
TAUPO
GISBORNE
NEW PLYMOUTH
NAPIER
WANGANUI
PALMERSTON NORTH
MASTERTON
WELLINGTON
NELSON
BLENHEIM
GREYMOUTH
FRANZ JOSEF GLACIER
FOX GLACIER
MT COOK
CHRISTCHURCH
TIMARU
WANAKA
MILFORD SOUND
QUEENSTOWN
OAMARU
TE ANAU
DUNEDIN
INVERCARGILL
NEW ZEALAND 1D 3D POSTAGE
20c NEW ZEALAND
NEW ZEALAND 1D 2D
1/6
5d 6d
2/6 NEW ZEALAND
NEW ZEALAND 3 POSTAGE & REVENUE 3
NEW ZEALAND 9d 1859 1959
NEW ZEALAND 4d
8d NEW ZEALAND 1862-1957
NEW ZEALAND 1D 4D POSTAGE HEALTH
50c

Dedicated Women

Here are those women from the Women's Division of Federated Farmers again. And what a stylish production of the logo – a lovely ribbon banner with tassels. A mighty number of 'ladies-a-plate' batches of scones, sandwiches, cakes, and even whitebait fritters must have been covered by this tea towel in every corner of the land. I've got two of them; the one seen here while the other has been sewn to make curtains in my kitchen.

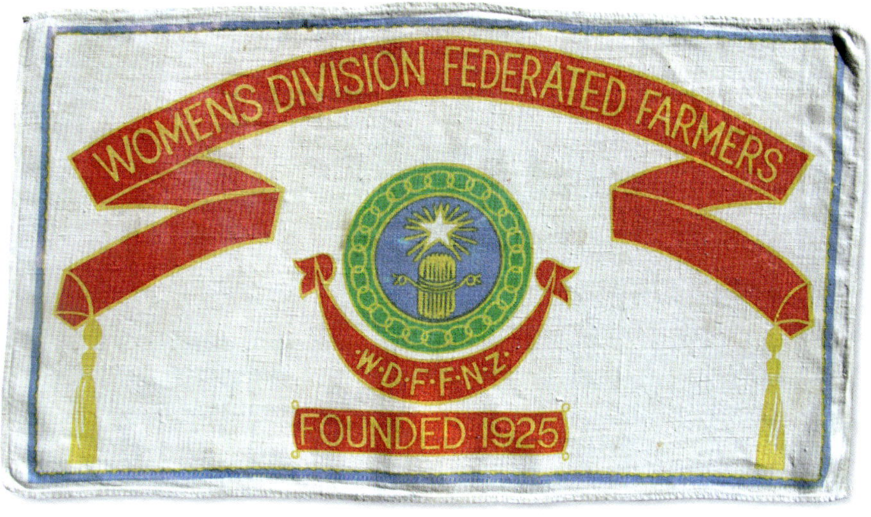
WOMENS DIVISION FEDERATED FARMERS
·W·D·F·F·N·Z·
FOUNDED 1925

Best of the Best

This is a pretty frequently sighted tourist tea towel that compares New Zealand with the rest of the world in a fair and even-handed sort of way. It points out that the rest of the world is dangerous and uninhabitable whereas New Zealand is simply a collection of the biggest and best of everything. Of interest to many men might be the inscriptions that locate the 'fastest girls in the world' in and around Kaikoura and 'the prettiest girls in the world' in the Riverton-Tuatapere area.

WORLD TOURIST MAP
EARTHQUAKES
DROUGHTS
SALT MINES
WILD CATS
ICEBERGS
TORNADOES
FOGS
BLEAK MANGROVE SWAMPS
BANDITS
WATERLESS DESERT
INCESSANT RAIN
TIDAL WAVES
WOLVES
VIPERS
TYPHOONS
POMMIES
DANK AIRLESS JUNGLE
BITTERLY COLD
FROZEN WILDERNESS
SWAMPS
UNBEARABLY HOT
FEVER BELT
VAMPIRES
INFESTED SWAMPS
MAD BULLS
RUINS
FLOODS
WARLIKE TRIBES
POLLUTED POND
DISASTER AREA
EARTHQUAKES
BRIGANDS
MAN-EATING TIGERS
HEAD HUNTERS
PIRATES
SNAKES
GIANT RATS
SHARKS
WILD DOGS
MAD DOGS
HOT DOGS
COBRAS
CYCLONES
ANGRY LIONS
ANGRY ELEPHANTS
ANGRY VISITORS
TIGERS
MALARIA
FEVER COAST
POISONOUS JELLYFISH
LEECHES
SEA SNAKES
WILD ANIMALS
WILD MEN
WILD WOMEN
TIGERS
CANNIBALS
TYPHOONS
STORMS
HURRICANES
SHARKS
TSETSE FLIES
FOG
Uncharted desert island off N.Z. populated by a backward tribe known as STRINES
SHARKS
NOTHING!
SHARKS
SCORPIONS
TRACKLESS WASTE
ROCKS
MAMBAS
VENOMOUS SNAKES
SHARKS
BLIZZARDS
Shaded area shows coastal mud flats
VIOLENT STORMS
INCESSANT STORMS
FROZEN WASTE
HAMBURGERS
DESERT TWISTERS
WILD DOGS
HOT DOGS
TIDAL WAVES
BANDITS
FEVER COAST
GIANT SNAKES
HOSTILE INDIANS
WILD JAGUARS
BLOWGUNS
BEST FISHING - in the WORLD
LONGEST BEACHES - in the WORLD
FINEST CLIMATE - in the WORLD
BLUEST SEA - in the WORLD
FINEST HARBOURS - in the WORLD
BEST SURFING BEACHES - in the WORLD
CALMEST SEA - in the WORLD
BEST YACHTING - in the WORLD
FRESHEST SEA AIR
GENTLEST BREEZES
FINEST SHOOTING
MOST GAME BIRDS
MOST FISH - in the WORLD
SAFEST SWIMMING - in the WORLD
MOST SUNSHINE - in the WORLD
BIGGEST FISH - in the WORLD
MOST BEAUTIFUL COASTLINE - in the WORLD
FINEST CITY in the WORLD
BEST HOT POOLS
BEST WATER SPORT in the WORLD
WEAKEST WOMEN - in the WORLD
BEAUTIFUL MERMAIDS
SANDIEST BEACHES in the WORLD
STRONGEST MEN - in the WORLD
CHEAPEST HOTELS in the WORLD
FRIENDLY MERMAIDS
STRONGEST BEER in the WORLD
FINEST LAKES in the WORLD
CALMEST FERRY CROSSING in the WORLD
BEST TROUT FISHING in the WORLD
MOST TROUT in the WORLD
BIGGEST TROUT in the WORLD
SUNNIEST COAST - in the WORLD
FINEST WATER SKI-ING in the WORLD
VERY FRIENDLY MERMAIDS
MOST PLAYFUL DOLPHINS in the WORLD
MUDDIEST BOILING MUD in the WORLD
FRIENDLIEST AREA in the WORLD
SAFEST ACTIVE VOLCANOES in the WORLD
FINEST THERMAL ZONE in the WORLD
MOST PUBS in the WORLD
MOST ACTIVE VOLCANOES in the WORLD
BEST BEER in the WORLD
BEST BOATING FISHING SURFING & SWIMMING COAST
BIGGEST APPLES in the WORLD
MOST APRICOTS in the WORLD
BEST GOVERNMENT in the WORLD
FINEST HOT AIR FACTORY in the WORLD
MOST FANTASTIC FIORDS in the WORLD
FASTEST GIRLS in the WORLD
MOST IMPRESSIVE SCENIC VIEWS in the WORLD
HIGHEST MOUNTAINS in the WORLD
DEEPEST LAKES in the WORLD
DENSEST FOREST in the WORLD
MOST DEER & WILD PIGS in the WORLD
MOST MERMAIDS in the WORLD
LARGEST DEER & FIERCEST PIG in the WORLD
BEST (SAFEST) HUNTING in the WORLD
PRETTIEST GIRLS in the WORLD
HANDSOMEST MEN in the WORLD
MOST MODEST PEOPLE in the WORLD
New Zealand
100% COTTON
NEW ZEALAND COPYRIGHT N.Z. NO. 2018

Less is More

There's very little that I can say about this. It's well drawn, it displays a tasteful use of the colour orange, and obviously the boy has a real gift with a hammer and chisel – and it's altogether culturally and sociologically wrong in so many ways. But somehow it works; for me, anyway.

Greetings from
New Zealand
T. PUKUNUI & SON
MASTER
CARVERS
PURE LINEN
FAST COLOURS

The Good Old Days

I particularly love the low-rise street scene complete with trolley buses and hydrofoil on the harbour in this tea towel depicting these scenes of old Auckland. Hydofoils were the latest and greatest in the late 1950s and 60s, but to my knowledge they have disappeared from service everywhere. However Wellington still has its trolley buses, and good on them – quiet and fumeless, they are a brilliant form of transportation. But this is an Auckland tea towel and it's a really pretty picture of how it used to be.

Auckland
New Zealand
KIWI
AUCKLAND HARBOUR
QUEEN STREET
UNIVERSITY
RANGITOTO ISLAND AND HYDROFOIL.
WAR MEMORIAL MUSEUM
A GENUINE DEREK SOUVENIR
PURE LINEN

Treasure Map

The three men super-imposed on the map along the mountain range at first glance look like they are holding gigantic paint rollers. However, I think they represent white-baiters and their location on the map might indicate the top white-baiting spots. That information along with the icon of a man gold-panning near Kumara suggests this tea towel can be used as a treasure map of sorts. It misses a beat by not featuring a pile of whitebait patties alongside a bottle of mint sauce, surely the singularly most regional food combination that I'm aware of in New Zealand. In time, when the glaciers have retreated so far up the valleys no one can see them any more, this will be collectable as a fine example of a pre-global warming tea towel.

SCENIC SOUTH ISLAND
HAWKES CRAG
SHANTYTOWN
PUNAKAIKA ROCKS
KNIGHT POINT (HAAST)
HOKITIKA
MOTUEKA
NELSON
PICTON
BLENHEIM
WESTPORT
BULLER R.
CHARLESTON
PUNAKAIKI
GREYMOUTH
GREY R.
KAIKOURA
HANMER SPRINGS
L.BRUNNER
KUMARA
TARAMAKAU R.
HOKITIKA R.
OKARITO
WHATAROA
FRANZ JOSEF GLACIER
WHATAROA R.
CHRISTCHURCH
FOX GLACIER
COOK R.
BRUCE BAY
MOUNT COOK
NATIONAL PARK
JACKSON BAY
L.PARINGA
HAAST
HAAST R.
L.TEKAPO
TIMARU
L.PUKAKI
TWIZEL
L.OHAU
L.HAWEA
CASCADE R.
L.WANAKA
MITRE PEAK
WANAKA
L.WAKATIPU
ARROWTOWN
QUEENSTOWN
CROMWELL
OAMARU
TE ANAU
ALEXANDRA
L.MANAPOURI
ROXBURGH
DUNEDIN
MOSGIEL
BALCLUTHA
GORE
INVERCARGILL
MOUNTAIN BUTTERCUP
MT.COOK
MOUNTAIN BUTTERCUP AND DAISY
LAKE WANAKA
TITOKI BERRIES
QUEENSTOWN
FOX GLACIER
FRANZ JOSEF GLACIER
WHITE HERON SANCTUARY OKARITO
NEW ZEALAND
PURE LINEN
FAST COLOURS

The Lure of Caroline Bay

Timaru. The Sunshine City? Well, if you say so. I'm not familiar with that Timaru. The Timaru I know is the grey overcast, wet and cold southerly capital of South Canterbury Timaru. But here, in a tequila sunrise colour gradient, we can see Caroline Bay in the throes of its mid-summer, possibly New Year's Eve frenzy. In years gone by youths from all over the central South Island used to head to Caroline Bay on New Year's Eve to get up to no good. There they would listen to bands, watch the girls in the Miss Caroline Bay competition, throw bottles, and get arrested. The police issuing warnings for the youth of the South Island not to congregate there just served as a reminder for anyone who might be looking for a bit of spice to liven up their New Year's Eve.

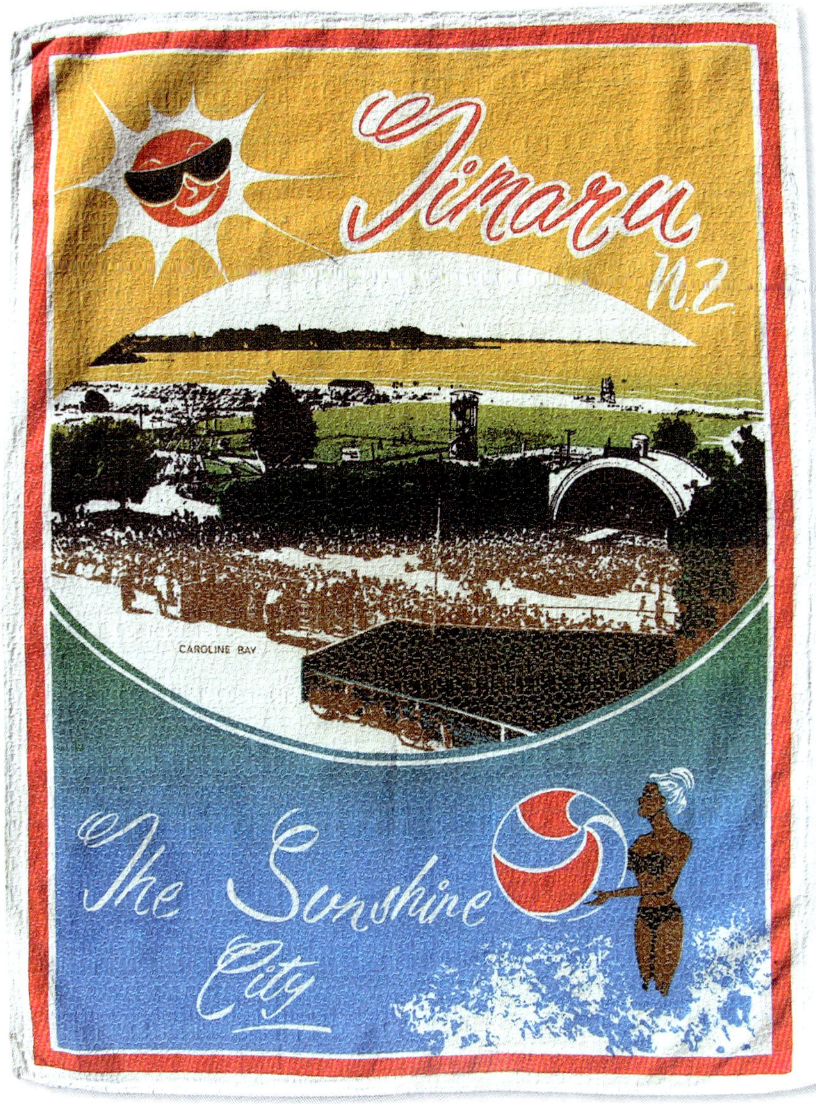
Timaru
N.Z
CAROLINE BAY
The Sunshine City

A Taste of Kiwi

Another tasteful tea towel from the Country Women's Institute, that bastion of every rural community. Beautifully composed, it features the Latin names of plants that I'm unable to recognise (I'm not sure what this says about my knowledge of things botanical). Note the cross-stitch kiwi here identified by its scientific name.

FOR HOME AND COUNTRY

New Zealand Country Women's Institute

Platyloma Falcata.   Apteryx mantelli   Apteryx mantelli   Scolopendrum Officinalis

Lazy Hazy Days of Summer

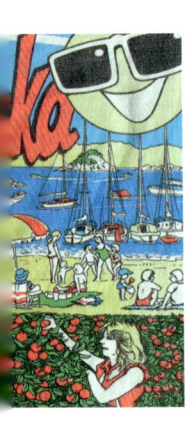

When I was a university student, I knew a girl who I would have liked to have called my girlfriend. She lived in Motueka and one summer I biked there, and then home again. In those days the fields around Motueka were full of tobacco and the town's man-made landmark was the clock tower, erected in 1950 by the owner of the local tobacco-processing factory, in the main street. Now restored by a local trust, it's been repainted but with no mention of its tobacco-related past. Motueka must have about the best summer weather of all of New Zealand, which is presumably why the woman on the tea towel has so many red fruit to pick. I suspect that the intricate two-tone crochet work around the edge was done by someone on a long Motueka summer holiday.

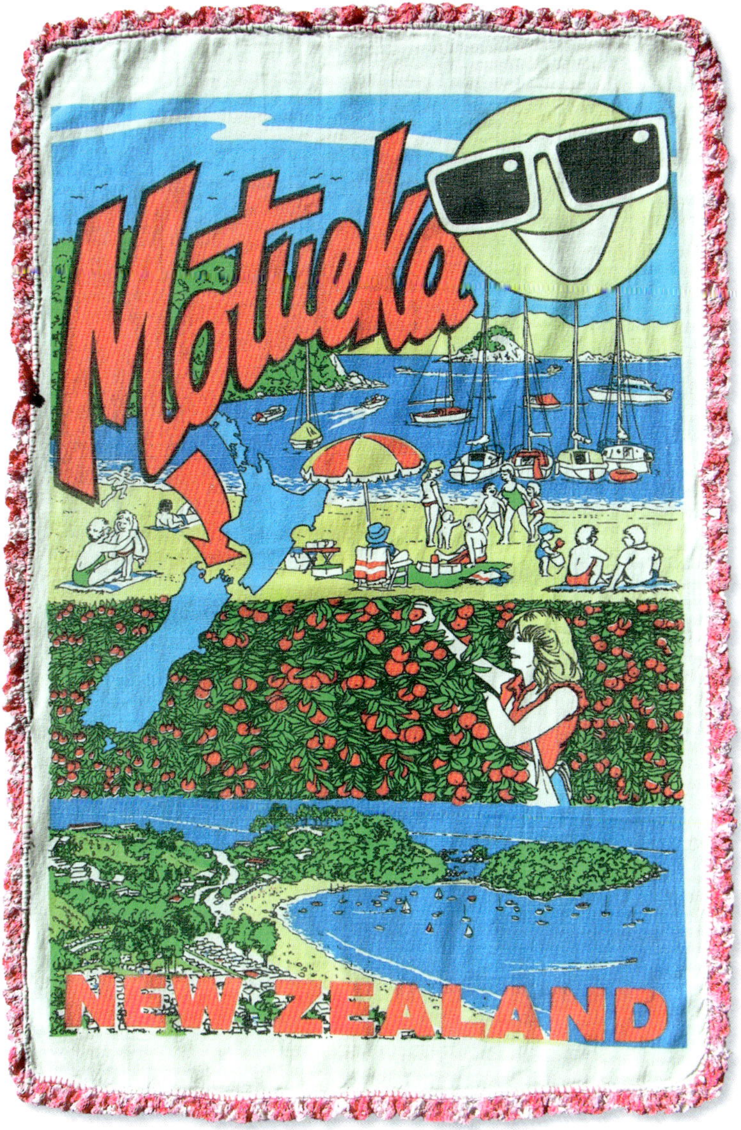
Motueka
NEW ZEALAND

Porirua North

This is a wonderfully bold tea towel design. And there's no mistaking where it's from with its great tiki, lovely borders, pretty flowers, fern fronds, map, swooping text and a busy kiwi. In short there's something for everyone. But I'm not sure what the gold coast thing is all about. I know it as the most western, or northern, suburb of Porirua and that it used to be a nice train trip from Wellington in the summertime.

PUKERUA BAY
Gold Coast
NZ
SOUVENIR
OF NEW ZEALAND
NATURAL FLAX LINEN NZ 2005
COPYRIGHT

Nothing for the Blokes

Here's another tea towel that was created to ease the transition to decimal currency featuring a highly educated kiwi standing by a blackboard with the conversions surrounded by household food items priced in both currency systems. Of more interest is the opportunity to contemplate the effects of inflation since 1967. Milk is an obvious place to start. A quart of the stuff cost 8 cents and a decent-sized snapper around 65 cents. I used to have another tea towel that showed the prices of stockings, lipstick, hairspray and related women's toiletries. But I've never been able to find a tea directed at a man who might want to buy a set of tires or a pound of roofing nails. I guess the decimalisation board thought it likely that a woman would spend more time with a tea towel …

1lb Lemons 1/6 = 15cents
Cauliflower
2/6 = 25cents
Cobboge
Dollars and Cents
Pennies
Cents
1d = 1 cents
2d = 2 cents
3d = 2 cents
4d = 3 cents
5d = 4 cents
6d = 5 cents
7d = 6 cents
8d = 7 cents
9d = 8 cents
10d = 8 cents
11d = 9 cents
1/- = 10 cents
2/- = 20cents
3/- = 30cents
4/- = 40cents
5/- = 50cents
7/- 70 cents
8/- 80 cents
9/- 90cents
10/- 100cents
11/-
12/- $1.
13/- $1. 30
14/- $1. 40
15/- $1. 50
16/- $1. 60
17/- $1. 70
18/- $1. 80
19/- $1. 90
20/- = $200
8 ozs Cheese
1/9 18cents
Quart of milk
9d = 8cents
1lb Tin of Peaches
2/8 = 21cents
1lb Potatoes
6d = 5cents.
1lb Butter
2/- = 20cents
1lb Bacon
4/11 = 49cents
5lbs Banana's
5/5d = 54cents
5lb Leg Mutton
15/5 = $1.54cents
2lb Oranges
2/8d = 27cents
2lb Fish
6/6d = 55cents
1 Doz large Eggs
5/6d 55 cents
28ozs Bread
7½d = 6cents

Getting What You Pay For

I ended up paying more for this tea towel than any other, the grand total of $106. Suffice it to say it was an auction and I became indignant that my first auto-bid was not enough. For some reason, the can of Swot Fly spray really caught my attention. Well, actually it was the Swot along with the can of Roxdale Apricots. I still find it hard to accept that there isn't a place on our supermarket shelves for canned Central Otago apricots. But I guess they'd still be there if we, the shoppers, weren't driven to choose our grocery purchases by price ahead of everything else. All this packaging will only come to look even more quaint as time passes, and with a spot of luck the price I paid will begin to seem like a bargain.

Marmite
Walls
ALL FLAVOURS
Quart
K
Marmalade
refresh
IGA
PREMIER
Raven Tea
Andrews
HEALTH SALT
Betty Crocker
FREE
all varieties
mono roll
LUNCHA
20c
Bluebird
potato chips
Wattie's
20 oz
PURE
MAGGI
SOUPS
SWOT
KILLS FLIES
Greggs
Sunlight
Family Size
Wattie's
SPAGHETTI
SUPER VALUE
ROXDALE
30 oz
APRICOT HALVES
FRUIT MIXTURE
CREST
baked beans
elfin
self rising flour
3lbs
Bell tea

More Than Just a Pretty Face

This beautiful tea towel has been used a great deal so the colours have softened with washing, which only adds to the beauty. New Zealand's indigenous culture rendered in linen, made in Ireland, it used to be the tea towel for which I'd paid the most and it caused me to pull out of an auction that I now wish I'd pursued. The auction was for a 'Rob Muldoon, not just a pretty face' tea towel, and when the price got up to the same level that I 'd paid for this beauty, I decided that it was somehow wrong to pay more for a single colour picture of Rob Muldoon's face than this detailed souvenir of New Zealand and Maori Lore, with its tastefully crocheted edge. Such are the bitter regrets of the tea towel collector.

Souvenir of
NEW ZEALAND
and
MAORI LORE
BOILING FOODSTUFFS AT THE THERMAL POOL
PATAKA FOOD STOREHOUSE
MT. NGAURUHOE, NORTH ISLAND
CARVED WOOD FIGURE
PU MOANA SHELL TRUMPET
MATAU FISH HOOK
MILFORD SOUND, SOUTH ISLAND
POI DANCING
HEI TIKI PENDANT
HONGI TRADITIONAL MAORI GREETING
HOTONUI OR TRIBAL HALL
TIMA A WOODEN HOE
KO MAORI DIGGING STICK
ALL PURE LINEN
FAST COLOURS
MADE IN IRELAND

Do They Really Like Us?

New Zealanders' sense of themselves has long been cast in relationship to the rest of the world. We always want to know what overseas visitors think of us and the biggest compliment you can pay a New Zealand restaurant, fashion show or hotel is to compare it to being in Italy, or France, or some place where they do things 'properly'. It's called cultural cringe and although it is now fading away, it's still evident in our national desire to be noticed and commented upon by overseas authorities of any kind. This old tea towel, showing sea and air routes, shows just how far away from the cultural centres of the world we are. I think it's high time we came to appreciate the value of our isolation and make a little bit more of it.

NEW ZEALAND
AOTEAROA

AIR ROUTES
LONDON - 12,831 Miles
VANCOUVER - 7,698 "
NEW YORK - 9,398 "
SYDNEY - 1,322 "
MELBOURNE - 1,496 "

SEA ROUTES
LONDON via PANAMA - 11,114 Nautical Miles
LONDON via SUEZ - 13,261 "
LONDON via CAPE TOWN - 13,678 "
VANCOUVER - 6,245
NEW YORK - 8,522
SYDNEY - 1,233
MELBOURNE - 1,481

Whangarei
AUCKLAND
Rotorua
Napier
WELLINGTON
Westport
Greymouth
Nelson
Hokitika
Queenstown
Timaru
CHRISTCHURCH
DUNEDIN

PURE IRISH LINEN   FAST COLOURS

Active Kiwis

What's not to love about cute cartoon kiwis playing sport? Although far from cute, I myself have played golf and rugby, and on occasion I still sail a dingy and play cricket, but I've yet to ride a race horse, or play lawn bowls. Having said that I feel more than a little bit connected to the world of bowls through my grandfather for whom the Clarrie Till Green was named at the Edgeware Bowls Club. As a child I would go to the season opening day for the afternoon tea, although my grandmother and I had to leave when the sandwiches and savouries run out, for that was when the old bowlers got stuck into the brown stuff.

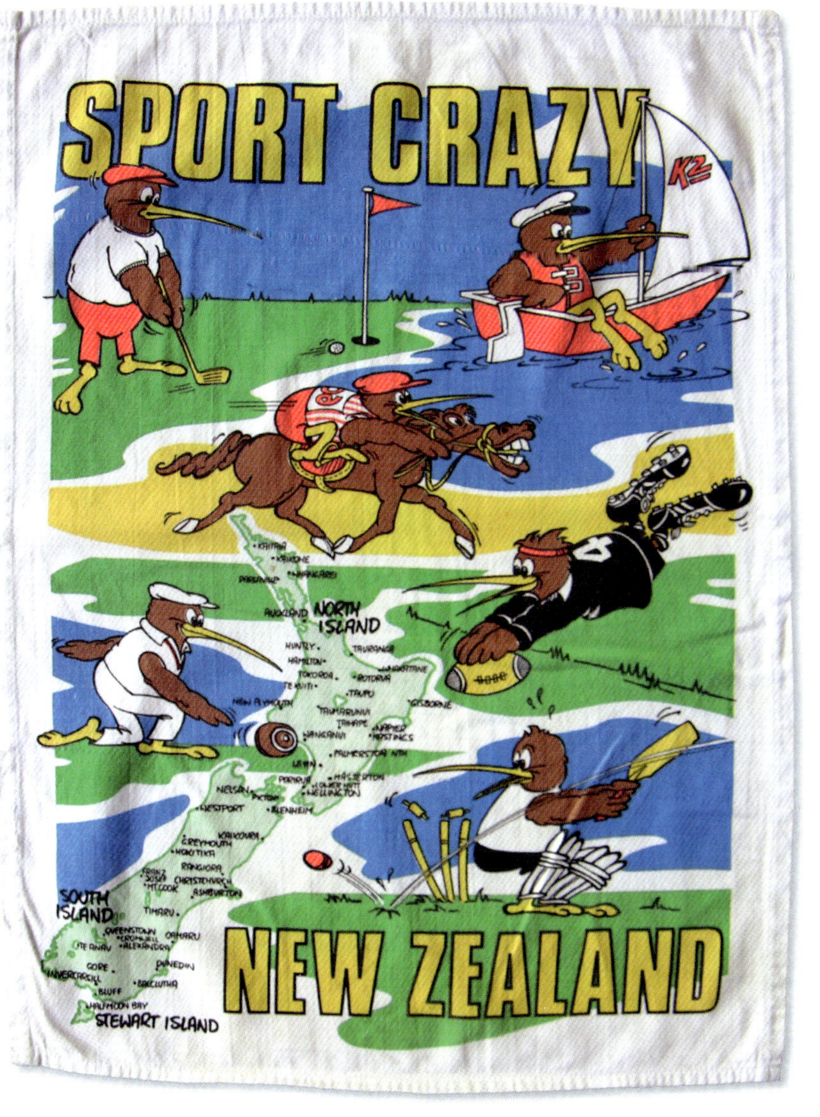
SPORT CRAZY
K2
NORTH ISLAND
AUCKLAND
HUNTLY
HAMILTON
TAURANGA
ROTORUA
TE KUITI
TAUPO
GISBORNE
TAUMARUNUI
WANGANUI
HASTINGS
LEVIN
NELSON
PICTON
WELLINGTON
WESTPORT
BLENHEIM
KAIKOURA
GREYMOUTH
HOKITIKA
RANGIORA
CHRISTCHURCH
MT COOK
ASHBURTON
SOUTH ISLAND
TIMARU
QUEENSTOWN
CROMWELL
OAMARU
TE ANAU
ALEXANDRA
GORE
DUNEDIN
INVERCARGILL
BALCLUTHA
BLUFF
HALFMOON BAY
STEWART ISLAND
NEW ZEALAND

Floral Tribute

The Home League of New Zealand celebrated its hundredth anniversary in 1983 and here's the tea towel to prove it. The League clearly had very close links to the Salvation Army in Dunedin, where the latter 'opened fire' on sin and sinners. The rising sun behind the house suggests there also might be some link with the Radiant Living movement. One thing's for sure, the Bible is big in the Home League. Very big, along with gardening, and commemorative tea towels.

HOME LEAGUE
NEW ZEALAND
1883-1983
'The Fountain' Dunedin.
Where it all began.
KOWHAI
MT COOK LILY
MANUKA
CLEMATIS
POHUTUKAWA
ORCHID
KAKA BEAK

Nothing Changes

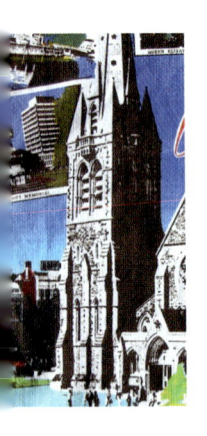

Here's my home town rendered in linen. The square has been redeveloped several times since this tea towel was printed, but everything else is pretty much the same, although the picture of QE2 park has it packed with people (must have been taken at the Commonwealth Games in 1974; I was there the day Dick Taylor won the 10,000 metre gold). I doubt it's been filled since. The airport, pictured just in front of QE2, is still there, lurking behind a big new three-quarters-built one and about to be torn down. There's a lot to like about the colour here. It's the tea towel version of what the world looks when you're tweaked.

AVON RIVER
QUEEN ELIZABETH PARK
INTERNATIONAL AIRPORT
CAPT SCOTT MEMORIAL
Christchurch
NEW ZEALAND
CATHEDRAL SQUARE

We're Lovin' It

It's always good to learn more about the ingredients that feature in our favourite meals. Here's an informative and stylish guide to beef cuts in tea towel form. And although I'm lovin' the font used for the numbers identifying the various bits of the beast, I can't place the source of the names of these cuts, especially Cut 16: The Clod. It's clear that the cuts on charts such as these vary according to their origin.

GUIDE to BEEF

1 SIRLOIN is the traditional English joint, known as the king of joints, it is finest roasted.

2 RUMP STEAK should not be roasted, it is very flavoursome.

3 BACK RIBS is prime quality roasting cut best cooked slowly.

4 TOP RIBS These have less bone than fore rib and are good roasted.

5 RIBS Have an average cut, ranging from 4 lb. - 12 lb. in weight.

6 FORE-RIB A large cut, cooked either on the bone, or boned and rolled.

7 WING RIB This is a large joint and one of the more expensive cuts.

8 CHUCK The best type of braising steak, should not be fried or grilled.

9 AITCHBONE A good value for braising or using in casseroles.

10 TOPSIDE A very lean boneless joint best for braising, can be roasted.

11 SILVERSIDE Mostly used for spiced or salted.

12 BRISKET Can be boned and rolled, for a pot roast, or eaten.

13 FLANK An inexpensive, rather tasty joint best for boiling.

14 TOP RUMP Can be roasted slowly but is best braised.

15 SHIN & LEG Inexpensive but wasteful, it requires long cooking as stew.

16 CLOD Can be used in many old stews and may be very tough.

More Than You Might Expect

Oamaru, Tourist Capital of New Zealand, is just one version of a range of tea towels that makes the same claim for a number of smaller towns. My mother's hometown, it's the place where you can buy the whisky once known as Wilson's. It's still there to be viewed in huge barrels in the old Dalgety Woolstore Building in the old town area, and can be bought under the Milford Label from the New Zealand Malt Whisky Company. I'm personally fond of some of the 20-plus-year-old single malt whiskeys they stock; just one of the many pleasant surprises that Oamaru has in store for visitors.

BENMORE

Any Excuse to Visit

This is the Queenstown of my childhood. Autumn colours, the hydro-foil and Coronet Peak. There's not a bungy jumper, heli-skier, un-finished hotel development or drug-addled foreign youth to be seen. I've been there quite a few times in recent years and cannot imagine ever tiring of the incredible spectacle out the aircraft window as we come in to land – and for that matter every way you look after I've arrived. All in all, Queenstown is a magnificent setting for the busiest (and possibly best) burger bar in New Zealand.

QUEENSTOWN
KAKA BEAK FLOWERS
NEW ZEALAND
THE SKYLINE GONDOLA LIFT
HYDROFOIL LAKE WAKATIPU
QUEENSTOWN
SKIPPERS BRIDGE
LAKE HAYES
CORONET PEAK
AUTUMN IN ARROWTOWN

You've Got Palmiers

I often demonstrate how easy it is to make lovely little crisp palmier biscuits with just one block of Fether Flake and a couple of cups of sugar. Roll out the pastry on some of the sugar to the size of an A4 sheet, turning the pastry between rolls to press the sugar into each side. Fold in thirds like a business letter, turn and roll out again aiming to get as much sugar rolled into the surface of the pastry as possible. Fold in thirds again and repeat the rolling out until it is once again the size of an A4 sheet. Fold the outside edges of the long side to a centre line, then fold longwise. Cut into 5mm thick slices and bake on a greased baking sheet at 200°C for 10–12 minutes, turning once.

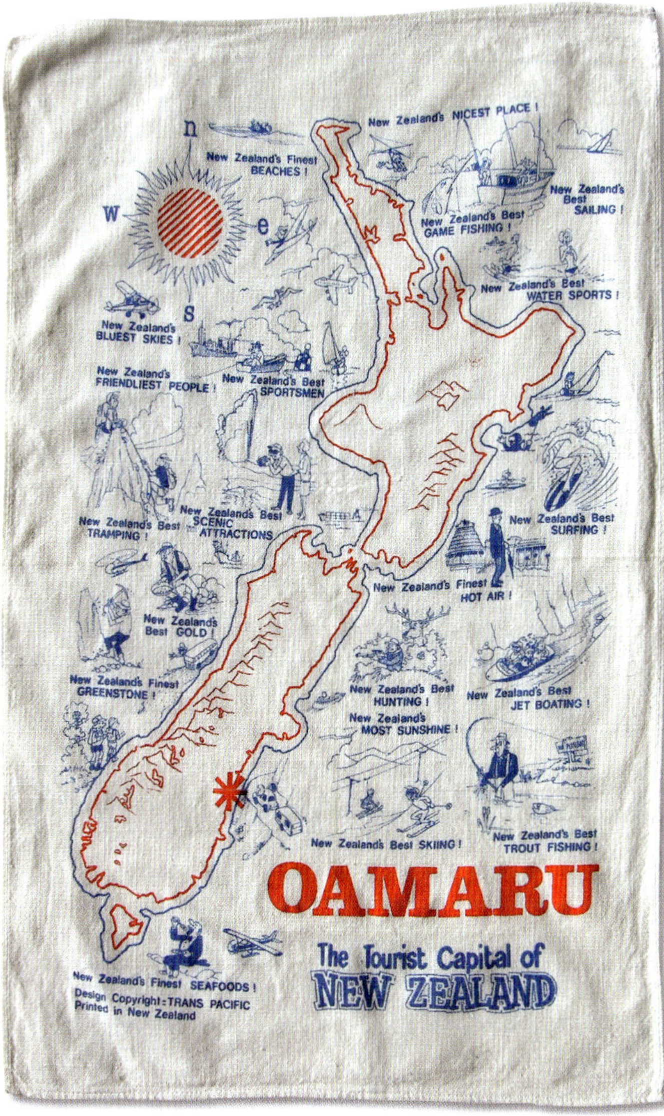
n
w
e
s
New Zealand's Finest BEACHES !
New Zealand's NICEST PLACE !
New Zealand's Best GAME FISHING !
New Zealand's Best SAILING !
New Zealand's Best WATER SPORTS !
New Zealand's BLUEST SKIES !
New Zealand's FRIENDLIEST PEOPLE !
New Zealand's Best SPORTSMEN
New Zealand's Best TRAMPING !
New Zealand's Best SCENIC ATTRACTIONS
New Zealand's Best SURFING !
New Zealand's Finest HOT AIR !
New Zealand's Best GOLD !
New Zealand's Finest GREENSTONE !
New Zealand's Best HUNTING !
New Zealand's Best JET BOATING !
New Zealand's MOST SUNSHINE !
New Zealand's Best SKIING !
New Zealand's Best TROUT FISHING !
OAMARU
The Tourist Capital of NEW ZEALAND
New Zealand's Finest SEAFOODS !
Design Copyright : TRANS PACIFIC
Printed in New Zealand

Be Prepared

Tatum Park was an epicentre of the Scouting movement in New Zealand. Countless boys have camped there, had their tent pitching skills appraised, their billy cleaning and camp kitchen organisation inspected and been marked for their ability to pack a trailer in a sensible and orderly way. Along with all that they would have spent many happy hours canoeing on Alligator Pond (bottom left), and sung a few rousing camp songs in Cooksy's Circle (centre left). Now Camp Tatum is a multi-purpose function centre, catering for weddings, conferences and school camps. One of the catering options is a BBQ down in Cooksy's Circle.

TATUM PARK
HOMESTEAD
SARGOOD BUILDING
WEKA
GATEWAY
TUI
TATUM
COOKSEY CIRCLE
CHAPEL
LORD BADEN POWELL
ALLIGATOR POND
UNDER CANVAS
SCOUT ASSOCIATION OF N.Z.
IRISH LINEN
Maylin
FAST COLOURS

Purple Prose

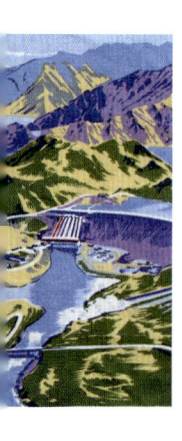

To my mind, this is the most beautiful landscape tea towel I own (the purple light on the hills behind the dam is a master stroke) and I was very happy to repatriate such an important South Island taonga from a North Islander who did not appreciate the significance of this piece of Irish linen. It represents a beautiful part of the country at any time of year, and the last time I stood beneath the dam it was mid summer, still, sunny and about 38°C. For the record, Benmore is the biggest earth dam in New Zealand, holds as much water as Wellington Harbour, and was completed in 1965.

ERNEST ADAMS

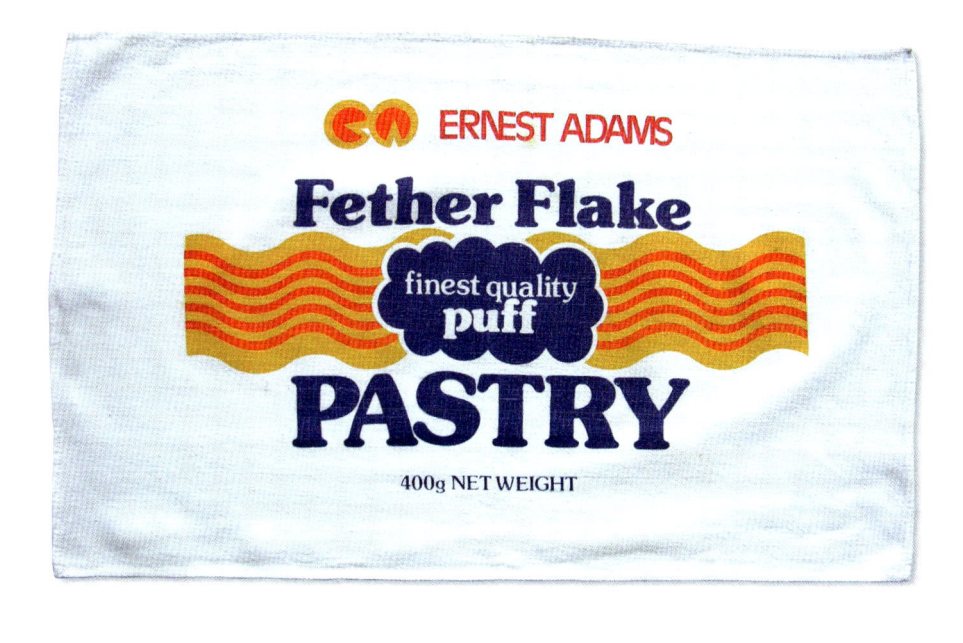

Fether Flake
finest quality puff
PASTRY

400g NET WEIGHT

What To Do in Nelson

Surely the squarest tea towel I've ever seen and featuring lovely vignettes of the city's scenic highlights. Everyone in Nelson seems to be an artist or craftsperson of some sort. Note also the crocheted edge of the tea towel, which prompts this useful tip for blokes. If the woman in your life ever complains that there's nothing to do, tell her she's wrong. When there's household linen without a crocheted edge there's always something to do! I'm certain she'll be grateful for the advice.

Fifeshire Rock.
Nelson Cathedral
Trafalgar St & Post Office.
Tasman Bay
NELSON
SOUVENIR OF SUNNY NELSON
The Haven.
Kaiteriteri...
Tahunanui Beach.

Somewhere Other Than Home

Another truly beautiful Country Women's Institute tea towel featuring a lovely tropical-looking idyll to contemplate while you dry the dishes in Gore with a southerly banging against the kitchen windows. It's a well proportioned design with its sprays of kowhai and clematis draped around a summer's day in paradise.

New Zealand C.W.I.
For Home
And Country
PURE LINEN
FAST COLOURS

Not Just a Tea Towel

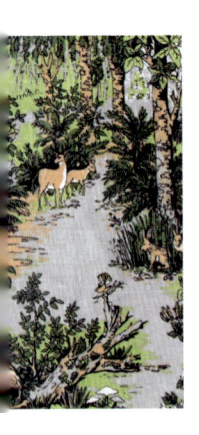

I've only just discovered this particular tea towel in my collection. Who knows how long it's been lurking there, undiscovered. It would certainly make a handy bush guide for trampers. Use it to wrap your leftover damper as well as for identifying the trees around you as you saunter along a very well kept DOC pathway in one of our glorious national parks or forests.

Haumakaroa
Kawakawa
clematis
Puriri
cherry Beech
New Zealand Country
NEW ZEALAND
NATIVE
FOREST
Womens Institutes
Wineberry
Wharangi
Titoki
Manuka

Wear Feathers at Your Peril

Could this have been designed by the Temperance League, Salvation Army or some other group with clearly enunciated views on the evils of gambling, drinking, smoking and women with big hats with feathers in them? A poor, long-suffering wife could clasp this tea towel to her breast (probably dabbing away a few tears at the same time) and through its reassuring presence remember that she's not alone. Her suffering is the suffering of her sisters. At least this is the message I take from the tea towel. It's possible I've got it completely back to front and it's a celebration of all those pursuits.

Where the Pounds go

Something for Everyone

More tea towel action from the months leading up to 10 July 1967. This time it's a shopping list showing both old and new prices. Notable to my eye is that three packets of biscuits would cost 45 cents, and a leg of mutton $1.54. Although I understand the illustration has been rendered in the naïve style, even that can't explain the tiny yellow bull with black polka dots. Never mind … I think I recognise the tree branch shelving unit featured here with vases and coffee pots from an old issue of *Popular Mechanic*.

Shopping List		
FooD	£ s d	$ cents
Butter 1lb	2'½	20 cents
3 PKT Biscuits	4'6	45 cents
Cornflakes	3'5	34 cents
2 tins Pears	3'9	38 cents
Jam	3'3	32 cents
Cornflour	2'½d	20 cents
5 lb Salt	2'2	22 cents
1 lb tea	6'10	68 cents
Black Treacle	1'10	18 cents
Oats	2'3	22 cents
Cocoa ½ lb	2'10	28 cents
6 lb Potatoes	2'6	25 cents
1 Lettuce	1'-	10 cents
Leg of Mutton	15'5	$1·54 cents
Bread	7½d	6 cents
1 Dozen eggs	5'5	54 cents
3 lb Sugar	1-10½d	19 cents
5 lb Bananas	5'5	54 cents

A Royal Let Down

Among other things this tea towel tells me it's only a few years until Rangiora turns 150. I hope someone produces a tea towel for the occasion. I only ever go to Rangiora when my soccer team has to play against the Waimak Rovers. We've a very good away record against them. In Rangiora's early days the Prince of Wales came out from England on a visit to Australia and New Zealand, and Rangiora was overjoyed when it heard he was to visit them. Excited locals decorated the whole town, a feast was prepared, a gigantic display of talented locals waited ready for his arrival – but he never came.

EARLY BOROUGH STABLES BEHIND HIGH ST. SHOPS

LOBURN FRUIT GROWING

ASHLEY FOREST

COAT OF ARMS

CENTENNIAL
Rangiora
1878~1978
NEW ZEALAND

MT GREY

RANGIORA

COB COTTAGE AT RANGIORA MUSEUM

TOWN HALL

BAND ROTUNDA VICTORIA PARK

ST JOHNS ANGLICAN CHURCH-1930 VIEW FROM HIGH ST.

ASHLEY-CANTERBURY TIMBER PRODUCTS

LIBRARY

FAST COLOURS

CLASSIC LTD. LEVIN N.Z.

No Place Like Home

Because I spent my teenage years in Dunedin, it still feels like home. I fondly recall those years of clambering around hills on the peninsular, the beginning of which is visible across the harbour (pictured middle left), fishing with rod and net, picking mushrooms or doing nothing in particular. A wonderful old-fashioned upbringing. Nice tea towel, too – especially the Star Fountain at the bottom left. I've seen it in action, but without benefit of the pharmaceutical assistance that obviously inspired the artist who painted this scene.

DUNEDIN

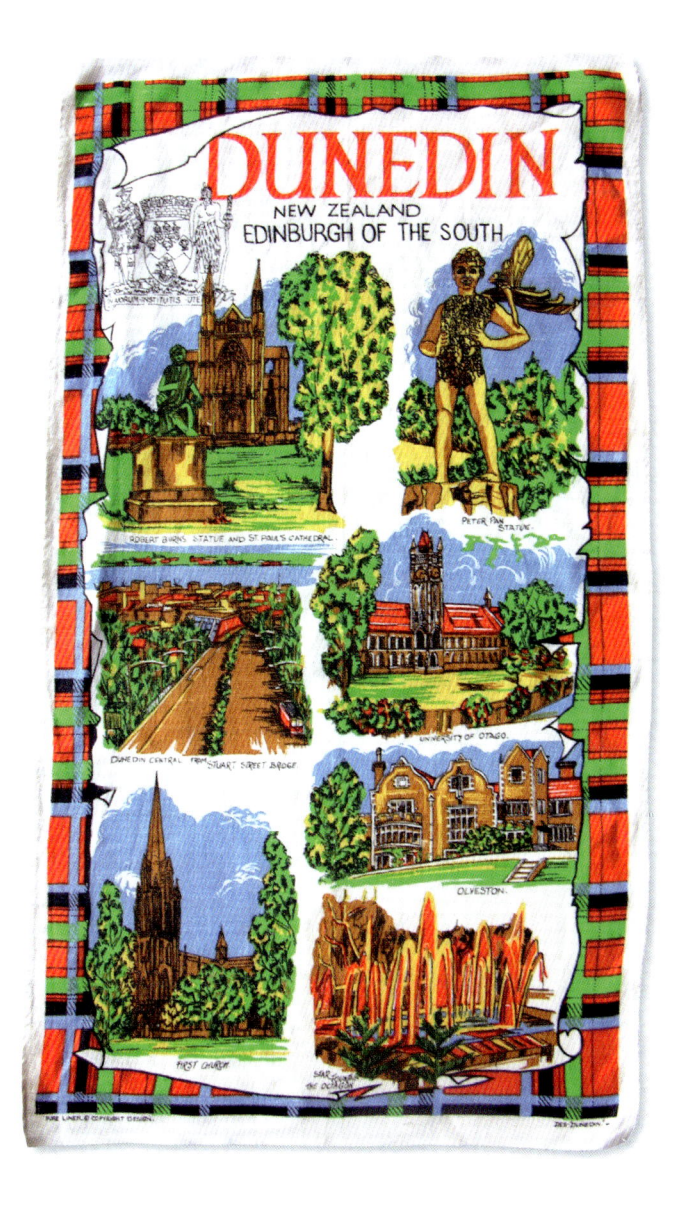

NEW ZEALAND
EDINBURGH OF THE SOUTH

ROBERT BURNS STATUE AND ST. PAUL'S CATHEDRAL

PETER PAN STATUE

DUNEDIN CENTRAL FROM STUART STREET BRIDGE

UNIVERSITY OF OTAGO

OLVESTON

FIRST CHURCH

Top of the South

Picton is one of those places that almost every New Zealander has been to, but unless the weather was too rough for the ferries to sail, or you were there in the 1970s when the unions were on strike yet again, you probably didn't stay there long enough to discover its treasures. My favourite Picton attraction, the hull of the *Edwin Fox*, doesn't feature here. Built in 1853, she had a long and varied life, even transporting troops to the Crimea. She finished her days as a coal hulk for the New Zealand Refrigeration Company in Picton. Speaking of ships, the ferry pictured top right, the *Aranui*, no longer crosses the Strait.

PICTON
NEW ZEALAND
Queen Charlotte Sound
NZR Rail Ferry GMV Aranui
Wishing Well
NELSON
PICTON
BLENHEIM
Marlborough Sounds
Pelorus
Excursion Float Plane
Picton Foreshore
Boaters Paradise
The Promenade
FAST COLOURS
PURE LINEN
CLASSIC LTD. LEVIN NZ

Picture Perfect

What a great note to finish on! A scenic beauty in which a kea flits amongst the southern rata at the bottom of the mighty Fox Glacier. It's a spectacular part of the world and this is as close as a tea towel can get to capturing the feel of the rugged mountain terrain. Sadly, the glacier has retreated somewhat since this tea towel was first produced.

PURE LINEN KEA BIRD **FOX GLACIER NEW ZEALAND** RATA FAST COLOURS

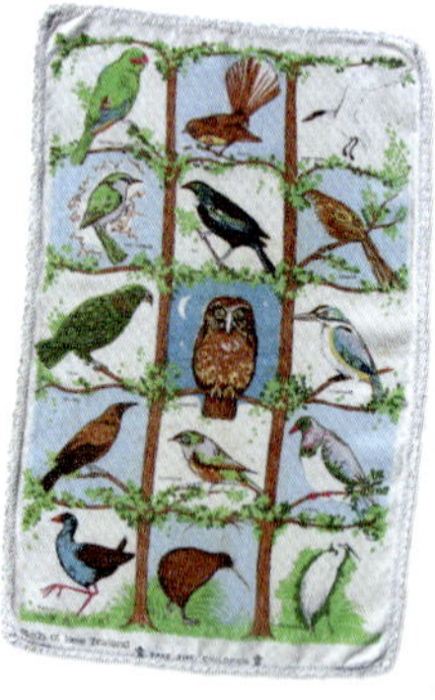